Here's what people are saying...

"This book is full of easy to understand and easy to apply common sense strategies on building wealth. Derrick's fresh perspective focuses first on internal wealth such as enthusiasm and integrity and concludes with prudent saving and investing ideas that are powerful in their simplicity."

— Richard Dolan, Principal, PEAK Learning Canada

"Derrick's book was a pleasure to read. He offers practical advice on creating wealth with peace of mind, but in a holistic context within an overall personal life plan."

— Douglas Gray, LL.B., author of the best-selling book, *The Canadian Guide to Will and Estate Planning.*

"Consistency of performance has always been the key to a great long-term investment. In Healthy, Wealthy and Wise, *Derrick Sweet has developed a holistic guide to consistency of thought and action that will help any investor to more abundant happiness and financial resources. Hopefully, the hard-earned common sense Derrick dispenses will become substantially more common across Canada as a result of his wise and inspirational words. It's highly readable and enthusiastically endorsed."*

— Phil Cunningham, President Mackenzie Financial Services Inc.

"Healthy, Wealthy and Wise *provides a practical, but entertaining approach to living and investing well. Derrick Sweet is well known as a successful financial advisor — now he can add proven author to his list of accomplishments."*

— Blake C. Goldring, President & CEO, AGF Group of Funds

"A refreshing book with simple, yet powerful advice on creating a different level of wealth. It's a must read for all who continue to search for a common-sense approach to living to the fullest."

— Tony DiLeonardi, National Sales Manager, First Trust Portfolios

Healthy Wealthy *and* Wise®

The common sense guide to creating abundance in your life.

DERRICK R. SWEET

Toronto, Canada
2002

Published in 2001 by:
The Healthy Wealthy and Wise Corporation
1 Yonge Street, Suite 1801, Toronto, Ontario M5E 1W7

National Library of Canada Cataloguing in Publication Data

Sweet, Derrick R., 1964–
    Healthy wealthy and wise : the common sense guide to
    creating abundance in your life

ISBN 0-9689711-0-50

1. Self-actualization (Psychology). 2. Finance, Personal.
I. Healthy Wealthy and Wise Corporation.   II. Title

BF637.S4S93 2002   158.1   C2002-900612-0

Cover / book design:
Karen Petherick, Intuitive Design International Ltd.,
Markham, Ontario
Printed and bound in Canada

Healthy, Wealthy and Wise is a registered trademark.

♛

Dedicated to:

Mom and Dad

For believing in me when I did not…

for being there for me when I needed you

and for your love and friendship.

It is an honor to be your son!

Contents

Acknowledgments ix

Foreword xi

Introduction xiii

Chapter	1	Your Mission Statement	3
Chapter	2	Goal Setting	11
Chapter	3	Persistence	17
Chapter	4	Integrity	23
Chapter	5	Enthusiasm	29
Chapter	6	Humor	35
Chapter	7	Confidence	41
Chapter	8	Gratitude	47
Chapter	9	Fear	53
Chapter	10	Life and Death	59
Chapter	11	Self-Mastery	63
Chapter	12	Mastering Time	73
Chapter	13	Savings and Investing	79
		Resources	89
		Suggested Reading List	93
		About the Author	97

Acknowledgments

This book would not have been possible without the wisdom of Karen Petherick of Intuitive Design International. Your knowledge and experience in book publishing has made this project a joy from start to finish…you have been an absolute pleasure to work with.

Appreciation goes as well to Dr. Louis Stokes not only for contributing the foreword, but also for taking the time to work with me for the past year conducting seminars and discussing many of the ideas in this book. Your insight and understanding of human potential has been a constant inspiration.

To my business partner and dear friend Catherine Friel, the most enthusiastic, dedicated and genuine person I've ever worked with or known. Every day I'm grateful for having you in my life…without your help this book would still just be an idea in my head.

To my good friends Gino Ciavarella, Gordon Corbett, Jonas Friel, Richard Dolan, and Robin Sharma. Thank you for your feedback, your support and your belief in me. I feel truly blessed to include you all as my advisors and mentors.

To my friends and associates in the investment community whose feedback and guidance was instrumental in the development of this book: Bill Holland, David Chilton, Terry Stone, Blake Goldring, Phil Cunningham, Douglas Gray, David McBain, Howard Gross, Kevin Nash, Richard Beeson, Ross Kappele, John Byrne, Wally Gabler and Frank Cianchetti.

To David Sersta, Executive Director of The Learning Annex of Toronto, who has given me the honor of conducting seminars on many of the topics in this book to the students of the Learning Annex over the past year and for providing a source for feedback on the philosophy of this book.

To David Aaron, my marketing assistant, your belief in this project, and in the philosophy of this book, has been a constant source of inspiration. I am lucky indeed to work with such a motivated and passionate person.

To Lori Rennie of Transcontinental Printing, thank you for your honesty, reliability and service.

And finally, thank you to my wife Marsha. Thank you for your patience, ideas and love.

Foreword

Derrick Sweet and I have co-led workshops for individuals interested in increasing their health, wealth and wisdom for a number of years. We teamed up to offer professional expertise to workshop participants who were eager to learn practical ways that would help them improve both their personal and financial lives.

Derrick is one of the most enthusiastic and optimistic individuals I have had the opportunity to work with. Always quick to see the bright side of everything, his positive approach to living is a source of valuable inspiration to every reader. In this concise book he presents the different aspects of living that he believes are important to achieve and maintain health, wealth and wisdom. His insights for improving one's state of mind are presented as practical tips for success that anyone can do.

The short chapters containing "common sense" information are of immense value, since they are meant to move you to action. There are thought-provoking ideas and practical tips in each chapter that will help you think about your life from a different perspective, become more motivated to change, and take the steps needed to become healthier, wealthier and wiser. Following through with just one tip from each chapter can lead to important changes in the quality of your life and your relationships to complete the journey of life!

There's an ancient saying, "A journey of a thousand miles begins with the first step." This delightful book can help you take those first steps in your journey to the states of health, wealth, and wisdom you want to achieve.

Louis Stokes, Ph.D.

Healthy Wealthy and Wise

My quest for the knowledge, that actually began when I was a teenager, to become healthy, wealthy and wise found me reading all the classics such as Napoleon Hill's *Think & Grow Rich* and Norman Vincent Peale's *The Power of Positive Thinking*. It lead me to read the wisdom of Abraham Lincoln, Plato, Helen Keller, Benjamin Franklin, and of other great men and women of their time.

Since the beginning of my journey of personal growth, I have read over two thousand books on all types of self-mastery. I've read books about creating wealth, getting "more" out of life, time management, the meaning of life, and self-confidence, just to name a few. Why did I read so many books, what was I looking for?

I realized that I was looking for consistency. Actions or thoughts that when consistently practiced, allowed the individual to achieve the important things in life — health, wealth and wisdom. I thought that if I went back hundreds, even thousands of years in time and learned what the leaders and philosophers knew about success and failure, then I would discover the keys to unlocking my own potential.

I still have not read any book that contains all the answers, or found that *one* book that will teach me how to become successful beyond my wildest dreams. But, I have managed to record the consistent habits and behaviors practiced by many of the most successful people that have lived on this planet. And that is the purpose for writing this book. *Healthy Wealthy and Wise*, not only tells you what you need to do, but it also tells you how to go out and start building the life of your dreams!

Before you read any further, I should point out, that this book does not have all the answers you need to master absolutely everything in your life. And, it does not offer advice on diet and exercise — there are plenty of those books already available. However, what this book does offer is tried and true *common sense* ideas on how to move forward on your quest for greatness — whatever that means to you. It describes the habits and behaviors you need in order to achieve the success, abundance and expectations you have for living the life you believe you were meant to live.

What you will find on the following pages is based on thousands of years of recorded success. It will give you all the help and the directions you need to get to your desired destination *if followed consistently*!

Remember, you are the captain of your ship, the creator of your destiny — where you go with this treasure of wisdom is limited only by your imagination.

Good luck!

Let's begin!

Your work is to discover your work,
and then with all your heart,
to give yourself to it.

Buddha 568-488 B.C.

Your Mission Statement

We are on earth for a short time. All of us are born, mature, work for thirty or forty years, retire and die; this will happen to most of us. Some people are born into wealth and may decide to skip a few steps, but in general, we all go through similar phases of life until our death. Why do some people seem to enjoy such full and complete lives with abundance in health, wealth and wisdom, while so many others seem to go through life living in mediocrity, boredom and emptiness?

The research for this book focused on the questions many of us are asking about life. I wanted to know why so many people seem to be drifting through life without passion or goals. I wanted to know how to create a life worth living. James Truslow Adams knew the answer, "Perhaps it would be a good idea, fantastic as it sounds, to muffle every telephone, stop every motor and halt all activity for an hour some day to give people a chance to ponder for a few minutes on what it is all about, why they are living and what they really want."

To be truly healthy, wealthy and wise we need to develop a *sense of purpose* or *mission statement*. We must have a reason to get out of bed in the morning. I have learned that having a reason to get up in the morning, other than

Many persons have a wrong idea of what constitutes true happiness. It is not attained through self-gratification, but through fidelity to a worthy purpose.
~ Helen Keller 1880-1968

to watch your favorite daytime soap opera, is the key to living a more passionate life, full of hope and enthusiasm. Let's look at some of the most successful people in the world — they all have a mission.

Sir John Templeton, who officially retired not too long ago, had a mission to successfully invest in great companies and create wealth on behalf of his investors; Bill Cosby's mission is to make us laugh; Dave Thomas, of Wendy's fame, had a mission to serve great food; Michael Dell's mission is to sell the world's best computers at the most competitive prices; and B.B. King's mission is to play the blues (at the time of this writing he is still performing into his seventies).

The power of having a mission in life can be traced back to the beginning of mankind, but the wisdom of having a mission in life is best described by the Greek Essayist, Plutarch, "The whole life is but a point of time; let us enjoy it, while it lasts, and not spend it to no purpose."

Look at some of the most successful companies in the world today. Federal Express' mission is to deliver your package — when it absolutely, positively has to be there; Goodyear's mission is to manufacture safe tires; Ben and Jerry's mission is to make great ice cream; and Holiday Inn's mission is to give you a good night's sleep at a reasonable price.

What is your mission in life?

It concerns us to know the purposes we seek in life, for then, like archers aiming at a definite mark, we shall be more likely to attain what we want.
~ Aristotle 384-322 B.C.

How to Develop Your ...

Mission Statement

How does one go about creating a personal mission statement?

STEP ONE

Draw a line down the middle of a blank piece of paper. On the left side write down all of your qualities, values and skills, then list the important roles that are your responsibilities. Here are some examples:

- *Skills — listening, skiing, tennis, carpentry, investing, selling and learning.*

- *Values — good health, financial security, good friendships, spiritual growth and contribution.*

- *Qualities — a sense of humor, fun loving, adventurous, analytical, charismatic, confident, outgoing, resourceful, easy-going and responsible.*

- *Roles — husband, wife, father, mother, son, brother, daughter, friend, student, artist, musician, and whatever you do for a living.*

You may need more than one piece of paper to write down all your qualities, skills and values...that's O.K.

HEALTHY, WEALTHY & WISE ─────────────

There is no defeat except from within. There is really no insurmountable barrier save your own inherent weakness of purpose.
~ Ralph Waldo Emerson 1803-1882

Once you've completed the list on the left side of the page, take a few moments to review. After you review your list, turn your attention to the right side of the page. On the right side of the page write down five to ten activities you enjoy doing, or would like to enjoy, while employing your skills, values, qualities and roles. This exercise should tell you where your strengths lie and what is most important to you. It also should tell you what you are here to do — your purpose!

STEP TWO

Are you ready to write your mission statement? There are no rules to follow; it can be as simple as one line or as long as two or three pages. Take another look at step one, while creating your mission statement, and be sure to incorporate your skills, qualities, values and roles. You may only refer to one aspect of your life (which should be the most important) or you may choose to include health, family, personal growth, career, and financial.

It is good to have an end to journey toward; but it is the journey that matters, in the end.

~ *Ernest Hemingway* 1898-1961

EXAMPLES OF MISSION STATEMENTS
The Simple Version — focusing on one topic

My mission is to be the best dentist that I can be. I am committed to learning all the newest techniques and developments in my field. I stay informed by regularly attending workshops and seminars to learn about the latest improvements in my area of expertise. I make every patient feel comfortable and relaxed during his or her visit by taking an interest in them.

The Longer Version — focusing on many topics

My mission is to be the best financial advisor I can be. I stay informed on the latest information in my field by attending workshops and seminars. I offer the best service in my industry, I meet with each client regularly, to discuss the performance of their investments and review any new changes in their objectives.

I am committed to life-long personal growth. I read one personal development book per week. I write in a journal each evening before I go to sleep to record what I have learned that day, and how I am feeling about my day's experience. I realize the power of recording my thoughts and I am committed to it for a better life and a wiser life.

Every person above the ordinary has a certain mission that they are called to fulfill.

~ Johann Wolfgang VonGoethe 1749-1832

I *am committed to health. I exercise no less than three times per week. I do not allow the stress of life to have a negative impact on my life. I eat only healthy foods.*

I *am committed to spiritual growth. Each morning I begin my day with positive readings that give me strength, insight and wisdom to meet the challenges of the day. I also begin my day with a 20-minute meditation. During my meditation I visualize my future the way I see it unfolding; I also thank God for all the abundance I currently am enjoying.*

My family is the center of my universe. They are my top priority. To ensure my relationship with my wife continues to be joyful and loving, we communicate regularly on our goals, challenges, and feelings. We always reserve time in our busy schedules just for us; nothing is more important.

I *am a committed and loyal friend. I support my friends to my utmost ability, they can count on me. I appreciate and enjoy my friends and make time for them.*

The road to happiness lies in two simple principles: find what it is that interests you ... and when you find it, put your whole soul into it - every bit of energy and natural ability you have.

~ John D. Rockefeller 1839-1937

Once you have written your mission statement, set it aside for a few days. When you return to it you will likely add other important roles, values, qualities and skills that you did not think of the first time you wrote your mission statement. Take this time to make improvements. When you are satisfied that the words you have written represent what your life is all about, go out and buy a picture frame.

Hang this "Declaration of Greatness" on your wall where it can be seen every day. It will serve as a reminder of who you are and what you represent in life. Each year when you review your previous years goals, review your mission statement. Go back and repeat step one and, if necessary, step two. Your roles will change, some roles will end and new roles will be created. Your values, skills and qualities will also evolve — you may even need a bigger frame over time!

The secret of man's being is not only to live but to have something to live for.
~ Fyodor Dostoevski 1821-1881

A man without a goal is like a ship without a rudder.

Thomas Carlyle 1795-1881

Goal-Setting

There is a common saying, "If you fail to plan, you should plan to fail," which is a reminder that there is more to succeeding than simply the writing of a personal mission statement. Many people do not take the necessary time to write out the "how-to" part of their life, and of course, without this critical piece of the puzzle most, unfortunately, will fail.

Going through life without setting goals and planning the strategy to achieve them, is like going sailing without the compass. Whether launching a new business or saving for your retirement, without a plan you are going to have a difficult time making your venture a success.

Goal Setting

It is one thing to make the statement, "I will retire at fifty-five with $2.5 million in investments to provide an income that assures a good life," but without a concrete plan to take you there, this statement is wishful thinking.

The key to successful goal setting is to look at where you want to be in a three, five, ten, fifteen and twenty year time horizons (or more) and divide your goals into bite-sized segments.

HEALTHY, WEALTHY & WISE ───────────────────

This is the only chance you will ever have on earth with this exciting adventure called life. So why not plan it, and try to live it as richly, as happily as possible.

~ Dale Carnegie 1888-1955

If Jane Goalsetter is thirty-five years old today and wants to retire at sixty with $2.5 million in invested assets, but only has $5,000 in investments today, she must plan out the next twenty-five years. The more detailed the plan the better. To break it down to how much to invest per week, per month and per year, Jane may want to sit down with her financial advisor and let him/her do the calculations using various "what if" scenarios.

You can apply this concept to other areas of your life. You may want to lose fifteen pounds. This is a lot of weight to lose, but one-and-a-half pounds per month for the next ten months makes it seem very possible to do without too much stress.

It is important that you have attainable monthly goals to bring you closer to achieving your yearly goals. I recommend you set and review your three, five, ten, fifteen and twenty year goals at various times of the year; you don't want to be overwhelmed with your goals, they should be fun to achieve.

The big mistake people make with goal-setting is they do it at the beginning of a new year. Everybody writes their goals/New Year's resolutions in January. We all know that the majority of people break their resolutions after a few months into the new year. Setting and reviewing your goals in different months creates a mood outside the mood of new years resolutions. Pick a day to review your big goals on a day that is special to you. Your birthday or your anniversary may be most suitable.

HEALTHY, WEALTHY & WISE

Those who cannot tell what they desire or expect, still sigh and struggle with indefinite thoughts and vast wishes.

~ Ralph Waldo Emerson 1803-1882

STRATEGY

Your strategy is to your goals what a recipe is to a great meal! It is a living, breathing part of your goals.

It's one thing to write down that you want to have a new car and $15,000 in additional investments at the end of the year but without a strategy the odds are it won't happen. A strategy acts as your game plan. You can start implementing your strategy immediately after writing down your goals.

Let's say over the next three months or twelve weeks, your goal is to lose six pounds and exercise thirty-six times. At first glance that's a lofty goal. It's not so lofty if we break the goal down into steps.

First step: Bring out your organizer and block off specific time to work out three times per week for the next twelve weeks. These are appointments that you have made with yourself and they *cannot* be cancelled unless something very important comes up.

Step two: Break your goal of losing six pounds into smaller goals of two pounds per month. Your strategy might be to vary your workouts into three different thirty minute exercises: running on Monday, using the treadmill on Wednesday, and the stair climber on Friday.

HEALTHY, WEALTHY & WISE ————————————

One day Alice came to a fork in the road and saw a Cheshire cat in a tree. Which road do I take? she asked. Where do you want to go? was his response. I don't know, Alice answered. Then, said the cat, it doesn't matter.
~ Lewis Carroll 1832-1898

How to Develop the Habit of ...

Goal Setting

STEP ONE

Finish writing your mission statement before you begin to write your goals. Once it is completed you can refer to it for inspiration as you begin to set your goals.

It is important to have goals in all the most important areas of your life. These areas may include: family, career, financial, health and fitness, social, special interest, relationships and personal growth.

Your goals should be big enough to allow you to believe you will be successful. You also should have long term (twenty year) medium term (five to ten year) and short term (one to five year) goals in each of these areas. Goals without deadlines are nothing more than wishful thoughts.

List all your goals for each category. Although there is no magic formula for setting goals, I suggest you start out with your long terms goals, followed by your medium and short term goals. Because this exercise is such a life booster, do it in an inspirational environment. Do you have a favorite place that is private and quiet? I often take a special weekend trip to write and review my goals.

After you have had a chance to set new goals for yourself, take the time to review them.

Never look down to test the ground before taking your next step; only those who keep their eye fixed on the far horizon will find their right road.
    ~ Dag Hammarskjold 1905-1961

Ask yourself the following questions:

- Are these goals realistic?

- Are these goals going to take me where I want to go?

- Are the deadlines for completing my goals realistic?

- Do I possess the skills necessary to achieve these goals, if not what can I do today to begin to develop these skills?

STEP TWO

The "How To" part of Goal Setting

The time has arrived for you to put your goals into action. Your strategy will act as the blueprint to make your goals happen; it will serve as the "how-to" part of your goal planning system. Write down exactly what you are going to do to achieve each goal. Goals become easier when broken down into bite-sized pieces. For the long and medium term goals, break down the activity required for each goal on a weekly, monthly, quarterly or semi-annual basis. Only you know how often you will need to chip away at each goal to make it happen. Block off time in your organizer, and stick to it!

The first step towards getting somewhere is to decide that you are not going to stay where you are.

~ John Pierpont Morgan 1837-1913

*Patience and perseverance have
a magical effect before which
difficulties disappear
and obstacles vanish.*

John Quincy Adams 1767-1848

Persistence

When you have completed your mission statement and written down your goals, the next step is to develop a habit that will give you the ability to keep fighting towards those goals, even when it seems that they appear impossible to achieve.

Persistence is the ability to persevere when others would have quit. People who persist have a vision, they have written a mission statement, they have clearly defined goals and a strategy to achieve their goals. They know where they are going and they are committed to getting there, no matter what.

It is persistence that takes a runner through a twenty-six mile marathon, and it is persistence that turns an idea into a thriving business.

Let's look at history over the last several centuries. When we study the lives of successful businessmen and women, politicians, religious leaders, actors, athletes, or any worthwhile profession, it becomes obvious that one of the most common personality traits they shared was the ability to persist in the face of failure.

We cannot help but think of Abraham Lincoln when discussing persistence. If anyone had reason to give up

If People only knew how hard I work to gain my mastery, it wouldn't seem so wonderful at all.

~ Michelangelo 1474-1564

Lincoln did. The following list contains some of the reasons why Lincoln could have given up:

* In 1831 his business failed
* In 1832 he failed in politics
* His second business failed in 1833
* His fiancée died in 1835
* He had a nervous breakdown in 1836
* In 1843 he ran for congress and lost
* He ran for congress again, in 1848, and failed
* He ran for Senate in 1855 and lost
* In 1856 he ran for Vice President of the United States and lost

But, he *never* gave up — he persisted. In 1860 Abraham Lincoln became the 16th President of the United States of America.

Colonel Sanders, of Kentucky Fried Chicken fame, now known simply as KFC, was rejected by more than one thousand restaurant owners to invest in his recipe for cooking chicken. He persisted and now KFC is currently one of the most successful restaurant chains in the world.

Thomas A. Edison, with less than three months of formal education, used persistence to create the incandescent light and unlimited wealth for himself, after failing several thousand times before achieving success. When asked why he never gave up Edison responded, "You know,

Every wall is a door.

~ *Ralph Waldo Emerson* 1803-1882

I had to succeed because I finally ran out of things that wouldn't work." Imagine what we could accomplish with an attitude and persistence like that of Thomas A. Edison.

Persistent people also possess other qualities of health, wealth and wisdom, like passion. You cannot stop a person who is passionate about their goals. It is easier to be persistent when you are possessed with passion, accompanied by a burning desire to achieve your goals, backed by a plan, and guided by a sense of purpose and your mission in life.

All goals and all dreams have roadblocks and detours. Persistence will help you find another road, build a new road or walk right through any roadblock. People who have developed the persistence trait have come to the realization that temporary failure is just part of the journey; it is not the final destination. Temporary failure provides clues that tell us what works and what doesn't.

I do not think that there is any other quality so essential to success of any kind as the quality of perseverance. It overcomes almost everything, even nature.

~ John D. Rockefeller 1839-1937

How to Develop the Habit of ...

Persistence

STEP ONE

   Write a mission statement (see Chapter 1).

STEP TWO

   Write a plan that includes goals with deadlines
   (see Chapter 2).

STEP THREE

   Step one and two were easy. Step three takes commitment and dedication. Many people fail to develop the
habit of persistence because they don't practice this step
on a daily basis. Step three is visualization.

   Visualize achieving your goals every day. The secret
to developing persistence is to feel with emotion, actually
achieving the desired goals you're thinking about at that
time. See yourself in possession of the goal, whether it is a
material possession, a career goal, a financial goal or a
character trait that you wish to develop within yourself.

   You must experience through visualization what it
feels like to achieve the goal you are focusing on. It is quite
exciting to anticipate the feeling in real life that you experi-
enced while you visualized your goals. If you regularly
visualize your goals, when you do meet temporary defeat,

Continuous, unflagging effort, persistence and determination will win.
Let not the man be discouraged who has these.
                                    ~ *James Whitcomb Riley* 1849-1916

you are quicker to get back up, dust yourself off, and move towards your dreams. Who wants to be immobilized by failure?

STEP FOUR

Stay far away from negative influences — especially those that will try to convince you that it's impossible to achieve dreams. We all have these thieves in our lives. By no means am I suggesting you dump your friends or well-intentioned relatives; just be aware that it is uncomfortable for some to watch you achieve more than themselves. It makes them realize that they are not living their lives to the fullest.

Every failure brings with it a deeper level of wisdom, a deeper level of confidence to overcome the next challenge, and an opportunity to step closer to your goals. Colonel Sanders realized that if one keeps knocking long enough, loud enough, and really believes in oneself, someone or something will answer; and that someone or something is called opportunity.

If you only knock long and loud enough at the gate, you are sure to wake up somebody.

~ Henry Wadsworth Longfellow 1819-1892

The strength of a nation derives from the integrity of the home.

Confucius 551-479 B.C.

Integrity

At the time of this writing the word "integrity" is being used to sell just about everything from automobiles to financial services. What is integrity? To have integrity is to be honest, upright, and reliable according to most definitions. Someone in the possession of integrity keeps their promises and is, above all, fair and trustworthy.

The *Healthy Wealthy and Wise* definition of integrity is: "Do what you say you are going to do. Practice what you preach even when no one else is around, and the only one to report to is your own conscience." You do what you say you are going to do. It sounds easy enough, yet many of us don't do it 100% of the time.

What if we changed our perspective for a moment? Just imagine. How would your life be affected if you knew that it was going to end, immediately, if you did not keep your promises? Would you be more successful in reaching your goals? Obviously the answer is a resounding *Yes!* If so, how different would the quality of your life be right now if you kept all your promises to yourself and to everyone who is important to you. How would you feel about yourself? Would you feel more confident? Would you have more

If it is not right do not do it; if it is not true do not say it.

~ *Marcus Aurelius* 121-180 A.D.

peace of mind? Would you be healthier, wealthier and wiser? Absolutely!

When we act in ways that are inconsistent with our integrity, we slowly lose our self-respect and self-confidence. We may even justify being incongruent by telling ourselves that it is all right that no one knows how inconsistent we are, as long as we are the only ones who are aware of our short comings. True self-confidence, however, is created and maintained by the conscience (the part of you keeping score). You will know that you're a fake and will not have peace of mind, as long as you are being inconsistent with your true beliefs — even if no one else knows. The only remedy for this behavior is, you guessed it, to act with integrity! Take responsibility for your actions and your choices; be trustworthy.

Do you have integrity? Listed below is the "Integrity Grid™," which will give you a better idea of where you stand and what, if any, areas need improvement. Answer the questions yes or no. Give yourself ten points for every yes answered.

There can be no friendship without confidence, and no confidence without integrity.

~ *Samuel Johnson* 1709-1784

INTEGRITY GRID™

1. Do you consistently tell the truth?
2. Do you keep your promises?
3. Do you admit when you are wrong?
4. Do you give 100% at work?
5. Do you give 100% in your personal relationships?
6. Do you not laugh at jokes that are of poor taste?
7. If you found a wallet with $1,000 cash in it and the rightful owner's identification, would you give it back?
8. If you witnessed a crime, would you come forward with information that could be helpful to the police?
9. Would you notify your boss if she/he paid you too much in your paycheck?
10. If your waiter didn't charge you enough on your bill would you notify him/her of the error?

Scoring: If you scored 90% or higher you have tons of integrity
If you scored 60%-80% you are on the right path
If you scored less 50% or less you need to work on building integrity.

The integrity of men is to be measured by their conduct, not by their professions.

~ Junius 1769-1771

How to Develop the Habit of ...

Integrity

STEP ONE

In your journal, list all the character traits that are important to you, whether you have them or not. After you have finished, review your mission statement. Are these character traits incorporated into your mission statement?

STEP TWO

Review your mission statement regularly. This positive habit will burn into the subconscious mind the character, values and life to which you are committed.

STEP THREE

Keep your promises.

STEP FOUR

Employ some kind of time management system or organizer to help you manage your time commitments. Successful implementation and follow-through will promote integrity.

Integrity without knowledge is weak and useless, and knowledge without integrity is dangerous and dreadful.

~ Samuel Johnson 1709-1784

STEP FIVE

Communicate. If you are unable to keep a previously scheduled commitment, whether it is an appointment with your dentist or a client, notify the other party as soon as possible. This action builds confidence in the relationship and strengthens your integrity.

When we have integrity something magical happens. Live with integrity and people, opportunities, and good fortune will be attracted to you — it's inevitable. Don't try and figure out this universal law, just live your life with integrity and watch what happens!

It is necessary to the happiness of man that he be mentally faithful to himself. Infidelity does not consist in believing, or in disbelieving; it consists in professing to believe what he does not believe.

~ Thomas Paine 1737-1809

Do every act of your
life as if it's your last.

Marcus Aurelius 121-180 A.D.

Enthusiasm!

A man or woman with enthusiasm can do just about anything they put their mind to. If this is so true, why isn't everybody enthusiastic?

Good question.

Enthusiasm is a state of mind and is very contagious! It is the ingredient necessary to see any plan through to its completion. All great leaders possess this quality and every great public speaker exudes enthusiasm.

Turn on your television any Sunday morning and watch the TV evangelists. One thing is for sure, these ministers are enthusiastic about their message and it is very contagious. You can't help but feel energized after listening to their enthusiastic presentation.

Enthusiasm projects your passion for your purpose. It's one of the most important qualities needed, when you want to influence and inspire others.

Enthusiasm allows us to carry on in the face of temporary failure. It is a power that gets you out of bed in the morning and keeps you working towards your dreams long after Joe/Jane Average calls it quits. It is your enthusiasm which creates a burning passion to complete all of your goals. Every morning when you wake up read aloud your

Enthusiasm is the yeast that makes your hopes shine to the stars. Enthusiasm is the sparkle in your eyes, the swing in your gait. The grip of your hand, the irresistible surge of will and energy to execute your ideas.

~Henry Ford 1863-1947

life goals with *enthusiasm*. Enthusiasm will never fail to inspire you and anyone else with whom you speak.

How to Develop the Habit of ...

Creating Enthusiasm

Not everyone is born enthusiastic, but everyone can learn to be enthusiastic by acting with enthusiasm. The following 20 habits will put you on the "high" road.

1. Get a good night's sleep. You know the saying, "Early to bed, early to rise, makes one healthy, wealthy and wise." And, you guessed — Enthusiastic!

2. Forget the junk food — eat properly to stay healthy. Avoid fat rich foods, white flour, sugar (pop, juices) and too much processed food. We all know a well balanced diet consists of vegetables, fruits and lean meats. Take the time to cook a real meal...faster isn't always better.

3. Save 20% of your pay. You'll feel more enthusiastic as you accumulate your wealth.

4. Be extra nice to at least one new person a day.

5. Always say "Please" and "Thank you" with enthusiasm.

There are only two ways to live your life. One is as though nothing is a miracle. The other is as though everything is a miracle.
~ *Albert Einstein 1879-1955*

6. Always smile when you answer the telephone. People on the other end can hear the smile in your voice.

7. Everyday, write in your journal the day's lessons and what you are looking forward to tomorrow. This habit will always nurture enthusiasm.

8. Review your mission statement every morning. It will reinforce, through your subconscious mind, the person you are striving to become; this will create enthusiasm!

9. Review your daily, monthly, yearly and life goals each morning. This will keep you on track and when you're on track you can't help feeling anything less than enthusiastic.

10. Tell anyone and everyone who is important to you how you feel about them — REGULARLY. You'll be amazed how enthusiastic they will be to see you every time.

11. Write thank you notes at every opportunity. The wonderful by-product of gratitude is enthusiasm.

12. Exercise on a regular basis. It's much easier to be enthusiastic when you are physically fit.

13. Read inspirational books on a daily basis. You can't help feeling enthusiastic about your future when you are continuously inputting inspirational information

HEALTHY, WEALTHY & WISE ───────────────────

Flaming enthusiasm, backed up by horse sense and persistence, is the quality that most frequently makes for success.
                                    ~ Dale Carnegie 1888-1955

into your conscious and subconscious mind.

14. Listen to feel-good music — it invigorates the soul!

15. Anytime you are performing a task or taking part in an activity, whether it be watching a sporting event or eating a particular type of food, try to imagine that this will be the only time you will ever enjoy this event. This exercise will introduce you to a level of enthusiasm like no other, and remind you, each time you do this exercise, how wonderful life really is. It will also show you how to focus on "living in the moment."

Create and write the next five habits on your own. You will feel enthusiastic after adding your personal input to this book.

16. _____

_____

_____

_____

17. _____

_____

_____

_____

A man can succeed at almost anything for which he has unlimited enthusiasm.

~ Charles M. Schwab 1862-1939

18. _____
    _____
    _____
    _____

19. _____
    _____
    _____
    _____

20. _____
    _____
    _____
    _____

This list doesn't have to end at twenty. You can create your own book of enthusiasm by adding each day to the original list of twenty to create several hundred or even thousands! What a resource you will have created to share with your family and colleagues!

When a man dies, if he can pass enthusiasm along to his children, he has left them an estate of incalculable value.

~ Thomas Edison 1847-1931

Imagination was given to man
to compensate for what he is not,
and a sense of humor
to console him for what he is.

Francis Bacon 1561-1626

Humor

Regardless of our position in life, we all strive to be happy, yet so many of us seem to be unhappy much of the time. Why? There are as many answers to this question as there are people. I certainly don't claim to have even half of the answers; but I do have a simple suggestion — LAUGH! Try it, go ahead, laugh. It makes you feel great, eases tension and will make you happy.

When I'm around my parents, Betty and Ray Sweet, we laugh a lot of the time. It seems that we often find humor in everyday situations. I love to laugh, and I love to make other people laugh — and why not? It makes them feel good too!

The mental health benefits of laughter have been documented for years. Laughing causes endorphins to be released throughout your body which causes a natural high. In Norman Cousins' *Anatomy of an Illness*, Cousins shares his experience using laughter as a medicine. He was diagnosed as being terminally ill and was informed by his doctors that he had about six months to live, and that he had a one-in-five-hundred chance of beating the disease.

For many of us, that would have been enough confirmation needed to fold up our tent and call it a day. Not Norman Cousins. He decided to use what life he had left as

HEALTHY, WEALTHY & WISE

An inexhaustible good nature is one of the most precious gifts of heaven, spreading itself like oil over the troubled sea of thought, and keeping the mind smooth and equable in the roughest weather.

~ *Washington Irving* 1783-1859

an experiment — he watched comedy movies, read comedy material, told and listened to jokes all the time. He was in constant pain; laughing for only five minutes, however, reduced the pain enough for him to sleep many hours. Norman survived his disease, and his book, which has been in print for over twenty-five years, is regarded as a must read in the medical community.

Today the world can be, at times, a pretty uptight place. Have you ever noticed the stressed-out look on peoples' faces on the subway, the bus or at public gatherings. I often wonder if they realize how unhappy they look. Obviously, everyone, from time to time, has bad days. I've been one of these people on the subway. Have you also noticed the complete and immediate change in physiology that takes place in these people when they laugh or smile? It's amazing! The next time you see someone having a bad day, whether it is on the subway, in a boardroom meeting or with someone you know, remember to give them the medicine they need — some humor!

Be simple in words, manners, and gestures. Amuse as well as instruct. If you can make a man laugh, you can make him think and make him like and believe you.

~ *Alfred E. Smith* 1873-1944

How to Awaken Your Sense of ...

Humor

STEP ONE

Don't take life too seriously. Remember, *you're just visiting this world*, everything is temporary, including you, me, and *all* our problems that seem so big right now. We all know that in a hundred or even fifty years our problems really won't be that big of a deal.

STEP TWO

The next time you are stressed out, whether it be at work or home, take a moment to see if you can find something funny to laugh about. Look carefully at what you think is causing your stress or tension — what would make someone else laugh about this situation?

STEP THREE

Watch funny movies or television programs. Go through your television guide at the beginning of the week and reserve time for yourself to watch a funny sitcom or, if there is nothing on, rent a funny movie.

HEALTHY, WEALTHY & WISE ——————————————

Good humor is one of the best articles of dress one can wear in society.
                    ~ *William M. Thackeray* 1811-1863

STEP FOUR

Spend time with young children as kids are naturally fun-loving. They love to laugh and they especially like to make others laugh.

We've touched on a few of the wonderful benefits of developing a sense of humor, but I think the American author, Grenville Kleiser, explained it best, "Good humor is a tonic for mind and body. It is the best antidote for anxiety and depression. It is a business asset. It attracts and keeps friends. It lightens human burdens. It is the direct route to serenity and contentment."

So go ahead and laugh or if you don't feel like laughing, smile. Either option is guaranteed to make you feel healthy, wealthy and wise!

HEALTHY, WEALTHY & WISE

Any man who has had the job I've had and didn't have a sense of humor wouldn't still be here.

~ Harry S. Truman 1884-1972

One never needs their humor
as much as when they argue with a fool.

Chinese Proverb

As is our confidence, so is our capacity.

William Hazlitt 1778-1830

Confidence

We live in a materialistic world. During the course of an average day, we are inundated with thousands of advertisements for everything from lipstick to lottery tickets. All of these companies are trying to increase your confidence in their products and services. What a great idea! What if we made up an ad for ourselves, selling us on ourselves? Doesn't this idea make sense? Who else stands to benefit from being sold on ourselves more than we do?

Throughout this book I have provided powerful quotes, many reminding you that you are the sum total of what you think about; what you tell yourself about yourself. Your personal ongoing commercial takes place in your subconscious mind twenty-four hours a day. It determines how healthy, wealthy and wise you are in all areas of your life. Have you ever said or thought comments like, "I'm always late," or "I wish I could do that," or "I'm not very attractive." All these mini-commercials are negative and destroy self-confidence.

Next time you see an advertisement for a product, notice how the company points out all its features and benefits. These companies don't just show us one commercial; no, they are continuously selling us on the strengths of their products, over and over again, with the

HEALTHY, WEALTHY & WISE ──────────────────────

There's one blessing only, the source and cornerstone of beatitude —
confidence in self.

~ Seneca 4 B.C.-65 A.D.

goal of influencing us to believe in, to have faith in and to be committed to their product.

A big part of who you are has been determined by the programming and conditioning you have been influenced by throughout your life as well as the dominating programming that you have adopted. At this point in your life your self-confidence has been linked to words and beliefs about yourself, that you have stored in your subconscious mind. Unfortunately, some of this data may have been programmed by negative outside sources.

Again, our self-commercials are running all the time. These messages may be conveying a recurring fear, an annoying physical trait, or a reminder of potential or past failures. This negative programming influences our beliefs, much like the advertisement for us to buy a product. It keeps us from using the thoughts of the healthy wealthy and wise.

All around me, I see people who are not sold on themselves. These people need to be sold on their true potential, the potential that each and every one possesses. We can develop higher levels of self-confidence by writing our own advertisements, by selling ourselves on ourselves!

Confidence is a plant of slow growth in an aged heart.
                                    ~ *William Pitt* 1759-1806

How to Develop the Habit of ...

Confidence

STEP ONE

Write your own commercial. Take out your journal and write a list of all of your personal strengths. If you don't have very many, that's all right; just list personal strengths that you would like to have.

Now that you have your list of strengths, go ahead and write your commercial. Here's a sample:

> Joe Brown, you're a fantastic husband and father. You are absolutely adored by your wife and two children. You are a confident man, who gets the job done. No challenge is too big for you, you can do anything.

> Joe you are an enthusiastic man. Your enthusiasm is contagious, and you make everyone you come into contact with feel fantastic.

> Joe, you are getting wealthier every single day. You're investing in solid investments regularly and dollar cost averaging into the stock market. You are an excellent communicator. You have great ideas and people want to hear them.

There can be no great courage where there is no confidence or assurance, and half the battle is in the conviction that we can do what we undertake.
~ Orison Swett Marden 1850-1924

This is just a partial self-commercial. You know where you want to go and you recognize the traits that you want to promote within yourself! Make sure you finish writing your own commercial before you read on.

STEP TWO

After you have written down your self-commercial make a tape of yourself reading, with unbridled enthusiasm, your self commercial. Listen to the tape while in your car, on your way to appointments, while getting ready for work in the morning, or whenever you find the time. There is something magical about the power of hearing the sound of your own voice telling you how wonderful you are. Listen to this tape every day for twenty-one days. You may even want to expand your tapes into specific areas of your life that you want to focus on, like your relationships, your exercise program or your career.

The commitment you have made to the principles in *Healthy Wealthy and Wise* will create boatloads of self-confidence. What lies at the core of your self-confidence is determination, desire, and a sense of purpose. Without these traits we would seldom venture to take any risks. We all crave this "knowing all is well" kind of feeling, and through participating in the exercises throughout this book, your self-confidence will THRIVE!

Confidence is that feeling by which the mind embarks in great and honorable courses with a sure hope and trust in itself.
~ Marcus T. Cicero   c. 106-43 B.C.

Assurance is two-thirds of success.

Gaelic Proverb

Do not spoil what you have by desiring
what you have not; but remember that
what you now have was once among the
things you only hoped for.

Epicurus 341-270 B.C.

Gratitude

We all have things going on in our lives that we complain about. Most of us complain about what is not working for us and what we don't have. Complaining about what we don't have leaves us with a feeling of remorse or emptiness and does absolutely nothing positive for us in making our lives more satisfying.

All truly successful people, who have total abundance, live with gratitude. Cicero, the Roman statesman said, "Gratitude is the greatest of all virtues." Gratitude focuses on what is going right in your life, it focuses on what you have, not what you do not have. Gratitude is absolutely free! Anyone can use it, anytime.

Gratitude will keep you from thinking negative thoughts. Practicing gratitude on a regular basis will eliminate negative thought patterns in your subconscious mind and, through a magnetic-like attraction, bring riches into every area of your life. Another benefit to practicing gratitude is "enjoying the now."

"Enjoying the now" is to be totally in the moment you are in, at any given time. For myself, as a young boy, I couldn't wait to finish high school, then I couldn't wait to finish college. Today, many of us continue this kind of "deferred living" until another time period, and then, once we reach

Thank God every morning when you get up that you have something to do that day, which must be done, whether you like it or not.
~ James Russell Lowell 1819-1891

this new time period, we defer again, until, finally we are at the end of our life, only to discover we have never really lived — how terribly sad. It doesn't have to be that way. Be grateful for today and for everything and everybody in it.

You can practice gratitude anytime, anywhere, but be careful — it is very addictive. Life surrounds you with things for which to be grateful. If you are reading this book from one of the G-7 countries (United States, Canada, Japan, Germany, France, England or Italy) you are very fortunate, and hopefully grateful too! We are among the wealthiest countries in the world, where we have peace, freedom and democracy.

Right now, take a moment to think about your own life. What can you be grateful for?

- *You're reading this book — be grateful for your sight. Every time I see a blind person, I am reminded how grateful I am for my sight and inspired by their courage and adaptation skills.*
- *Do you have someone who loves you? Be grateful for their precious gift of love.*

What else are you grateful for? What enriching character traits do you have, what skills are yours? Do you have a job, a nice place to call home, a car or just the clothes on your back? Each one of us can find many things to be grateful for no matter where we are in our lives and, in the process of being grateful, we will create the feeling of total and complete abundance.

HEALTHY, WEALTHY & WISE

Many times a day I realize how much my own life is built on the labors of my fellowmen, and how earnestly I must exert myself in order to give in return as much as I have received.

~ Albert Einstein 1879-1955

How to Develop the Habit of ...

Gratitude

STEP ONE

Think about your life. Go back in time and think of all the people who helped you become the person you are today. Make a list; think about the teacher who made a difference, relatives who gave you encouragement, friends who made a difference, authors who have influenced your thinking. Perform a ceremony in your mind, and thank each and every one of these special people for helping you — for making a difference in your life. Give them a handshake, a hug or a trophy; whatever image helps imprint the importance of who they are and what they did.

STEP TWO

For the next twenty-one days ask yourself, as soon as you awake, "What am I grateful for today?" Don't do anything else until you have listed at least five reasons to be grateful. Keep a journal and record your answers. Answer the question as it relates to your family, career, talents, character traits, friends, financial situation, health, and anything else you can think of.

Happiness does not consist in having what you want, but wanting what you have.

~ *Confucius* 551-479 B.C.

When I began this exercise several years ago, by day five I found myself being grateful for things I had completely taken for granted. I won't tell what they were; I'll let you discover them for yourself.

By the way, if you really enjoy this exercise, there is no reason not to continue doing it for as long as you like. Think how each day will start after this kind of spiritual rejuvenation!

Reflect upon your present blessings, of which every man has plenty; not on your past misfortunes, of which all men have some.
~ Charles Dickens 1812-1870

It is not how much we have,
but how much we enjoy,
that makes happiness.

Charles H.I. Spurgeon 1834-1892

Do the thing we fear, and the death of
fear is certain.

Ralph Waldo Emerson 1803-1882

Fear

The main objective in writing this book has been to provide practical *common sense* information about the positive steps you can take if you want to become healthy, wealthy and wise. However, if you harbor fear, are intimidated or immobilized by fear, you probably will not follow through with your life goals. In fact, you might slip back into your same old *comfortable* routine.

It's absolutely normal to have fear. Going back to the days of the caveman, fear ensured his survival. Without this *fight or flight* instinct we wouldn't have made it past the Saber Tooth tiger. Today we don't have to fight off wild animals, rather, we have to defeat our self-destructive thoughts. These thoughts can be just as fierce as wild animals and they can do as much, if not more damage, if we are not taught how to manage them properly. Once you learn how to tame these "wild animals" into puppy dogs, you will truly be on your way to becoming healthy, wealthy and wise.

Some of the most common fears we have are: fear of criticism, fear of poverty, fear of old age and fear of dying. The first step to overcoming fear is to develop an understanding and appreciation of it. Fear actually plays a very positive role in our lives; its purpose is to keep us alert and

It is not death that a man should fear, but he should fear never beginning to live.

~ *Marcus Aurelius* 121-180 A.D.

alive. Fear prevents us from taking *risks* like jumping out of moving cars, swimming with sharks, or trying to make friends with Grizzly bears when visiting our national parks.

Fear can also prevent us from taking business, social and personal growth risks. These risks are necessary for continued personal development. If we do not take these risks we do not grow. If we let fear keep us from attempting to reach our goals, the fear itself will grow. Eventually it can cause us to give up on our dreams.

The only cure for fear, is to *do what you fear.* We've all been there. Do you remember when you faced one of your fears? Do you remember how incredible you felt after conquering it? I bet you felt larger than life! Why? Because, in that very moment you grew stronger.

There is great beauty in going through life without anxiety or fear. Half our fears are baseless, and the other half discreditable.
~ *Christian Nevell Bovee* 1820-1904

How to Develop the Habit of ...

Fear Busting

STEP ONE

Write down all the fears you currently have. Be sure to include the fears that may be holding you back from attempting to reach your goals.

STEP TWO

Review your list of fears and prioritize the fear you want to overcome first, then second and third and so on.

STEP THREE

List the skills that you presently do not have, that you need to develop, in order to overcome your fear and reach your goals. What can you do to develop these skills?

STEP FOUR

Meet each fear head on. In life we are motivated, primarily, by two emotional states, pain and pleasure. We all want to move away from pain and find our way towards pleasure. Go back to each fear and visualize what will happen in your life if you don't take the risk and break through the fear. See your life five, ten and twenty years down the road. How has your life been negatively affected by letting

I believe that anyone can conquer fear by doing the things he fears to do, provided he keeps doing them until he gets a record of successful experience behind him.

~ Eleanor Roosevelt Roosevelt 1884-1962

fear get the best of you? For this exercise to work you will need to include as many details as possible. What do you look like? How do you feel? Are you successful? How has not taking the necessary risk affected your relationship with yourself and those you are closest to? How does that make you feel? How has not mastering your fear impacted your self confidence? Are you happy? Do you enjoy your life? What other details can you add that will help to complete the picture?

STEP FIVE

Now go back again to each fear and visualize how different your life will be if you take the risk and break through the fear. Look at your life five, ten and twenty years down the road. Can you see how your life has been positively affected. How do you feel? What do you look like? Are you wealthy? How has reaching your goals affected your relationships with those you are closest with? Are you confident? Are you passionate about life? What else can you add to make the picture clearer?

Remember, fear helps us grow. Each time we conquer just one of our fears, we gain self-confidence and in the process, we become better prepared for the next challenge in life.

HEALTHY, WEALTHY & WISE

The first duty of man is to conquer fear; he must get rid of it, he cannot act till then.

~ *Thomas Carlyle* 1795-1881

The whole secret of existence is to have no fear. Never fear what will become of you, depend on no one. Only the moment you reject all help are you freed.

Buddha 568-488 B.C.

Don't be afraid of death
so much as an inadequate life.

Bertolt Brecht 1898-1956

Life and Death

To truly experience health, wealth and wisdom in the fullest sense we *need* to talk about life and death, and how we can live more completely through understanding and appreciating death. Abraham Maslow understood the importance of appreciating death, "The confrontation with death... makes everything look so precious, so sacred, so beautiful that I feel more strongly than ever the impulse to live it, to embrace it, and to let myself be overwhelmed by it."

Many of us live our lives as if we are going to be here forever. We dwell on our problems, procrastinate, focus on the negative, waste time and rarely live to our true potential, until it's too late. I have come to realize that an appreciation of death can help us live our lives to the fullest. Appreciation of death can give us a greater sense of urgency to live with a sense of purpose.

The dying have often been among the greatest teachers of life's most precious lessons. When we are at death's door we clearly see what is important and what is not. It is also at this time when we see what we were capable of achieving, what our life could have been, if we allowed the greatness within to express itself. Everyone has this greatness inside, yet too many, take this greatness to their grave, never experiencing what could have been. We allow our-

Most people die at twenty-five and aren't buried until they are seventy-five.
~ Benjamin Franklin 1706-1790

selves to be immobilized by fear rather than motivated by it, and we continue to live quietly in the shadow of "what could have been."

I believe that if we keep in our consciousness the thought that we are only here for a brief time, we will live with greater intensity, we will waste less time on negativity, and we will be able to focus on all the good that is in the world. I *strongly* believe that living with a deathbed mentality helps you to live in the moment. You will see each day as a gift, you will have greater clarity on what matters most and you will begin to live your life as only you can, with a healthy sense of urgency.

Life can only take place in the present moment. If we lose the present moment, we lose life.

~ *Buddha* 568-488 B.C.

How *to Develop a* ...

Death-bed Mentality

STEP ONE

Imagine yourself many years from now at your own funeral. There are three speakers today — your spouse, your best friend (next to your spouse) and a co-worker, all of whom will give their eulogy on what kind of person you were. What will your spouse say about you? Were you a good spouse, a good parent? Were you kind, generous and compassionate?

Next, the co-worker speaks. What will he or she say about you? Were you a positive person to work with? Did you make a difference or were you just putting in time? Did you go the extra mile?

And finally, your best friend. What kind of qualities is he or she going to say you possessed? What did you stand for? What did you accomplish in your personal life, your career and for your community? Were you fun to be around?

Write down your answers. Take your time, this is your life you're creating; not just your death. Carefully list the qualities you want to hear describe who you were. Write down all the accomplishments that you achieved in your life including the following categories (feel free to add more):

Live not as though there were a thousand years ahead of you. Fate is at your elbow; make yourself good while life and power are still yours.
~ *Marcus Aurelius* 121-180 A.D.

Family	Married with two children.
Career	30 year success, achieved V. P. or Sr. V. P. or President level.
Health	In great shape, weighed X pounds, felt fantastic, ran three times per week.
Spiritual	Meditated once per day, took time out to regularly reflect on life, wrote daily in a journal to record life's lessons and challenges, always had a positive attitude.
Personal Growth	Was committed to personal growth, read one book per week, always had goals written down.
Special Interest	Hiked the Grand Canyon, climbed Mt. Everest, ran the Boston Marathon.
Financial	Had enough money to retire by sixty. Enjoyed an income of $100,000 per year at retirement.
Social	Had three wonderful friends and many colleagues and acquaintances.

Resolved: To live with all my might while I do live, and as I shall wish I had done ten thousand ages hence.

~ *Jonathan Edwards* 1703-1758

STEP TWO

After carefully listing all the qualities you wished to have possessed as well as the accomplishments that you wished to have achieved in your life, begin to meditate. Feel the warm feelings from all the people at your funeral; feel all their love for you. Meditate on your funeral for a few minutes, then go into a regular mediation for the day and visualize yourself accomplishing your goals and becoming the person you are aspiring to be, the person who earned such glowing commentary.

Great peace of mind comes from this exercise: you will be practicing visualization, self-mastery, and faith. You will also be conditioning your subconscious mind to expect to achieve these goals and to become the person you are aspiring to be!

Life is not lost by dying; life is lost minute by minute, day by day, in all the thousand small uncaring ways.

~ *Stephen Vincent Benét* 1898-1943

I count him braver who overcomes his
desires than him who conquers his enemies;
for the hardest victory is over self.

Aristotle 384-322 B.C.

Self-Mastery

Self-mastery, in theory, is simple; it means that you are in charge of you. If it is so simple why isn't everybody in charge of himself or herself and leading happier and more productive lives. Most people do not practice self-mastery because no one has taught them how. I certainly don't remember being offered Self-Mastery 101 in school. Often, we let outside influences like television, friends and colleagues determine how we feel and what we think.

The key to self-mastery is to recognize that thoughts have power. Whether you believe it or not, you are the total result of all the thoughts that you ever had. That's right — where you are right now in life has been determined by your dominant thoughts.

Now to the task of achieving self-mastery and controlling your life.

Have you ever noticed how a garden, when left unattended, grows weeds and becomes unattractive? Your mind is no different. If you let the negative influences in your life go unattended they will grow like weeds; only your weeds will look more like an out-of-shape body, lack of motivation, or poor self-confidence. Weed out your negative influences!

What you think of yourself is much more important than what others think of you.

~ *Seneca* 4 B.C.-65 A.D.

Weed Your Garden

If you have negative influences in your life, attend to them right now. Most of us, at one time or another, include ourselves as a negative influence. We may not be aware that we are thinking negative thoughts most of the time. Take the rubber band test. For twenty-four hours wear a rubber band around one of your wrists. Every time you think a negative thought, pull the band back and let it SNAP against your wrist. You will, before long, realize that you may have been unconsciously thinking negative thoughts.

Once you've taken care of getting your thoughts under control, take a good look at all the negative influences in your life.

- What kind of television programs do you watch? Are they positive and educational? Do you learn ways to live better, eat healthier, plan your day more efficiently, live with more zest? There are many television shows with positive messages, dedicated to helping you improve the quality of your life. One of my favorite shows is "Oprah." Regularly, Oprah interviews people who offer wonderful advice for improving many different aspects of our life, or she may invite people with inspirational stories of hope and what is possible...if you believe!

All the resources we need are in the mind.
                    ~ Theodore Roosevelt 1858-1919

- What do you read? There are so many *good* books. Visit your library or book store and browse the personal growth or self-help section. It is filled with books containing wonderful advice. Some of these books may help you find the wisdom you will need to absorb to achieve your life's goals.

- Who do you spend time with? Think carefully about this. Are your circle of friends encouraging and positive? If they are negative. I suggest you confront your friends with your concerns and hopefully they will see the light and move ahead, as you are doing. If they don't ... do it on your own, or go the distance by seeking out new friends.

Master your Mind

It may sound quite bold to say you can *master your mind* but it is actually quite simple. You have two thought processing systems in your mind: your conscious mind and your subconscious mind. Your conscious thoughts are those that you are aware of in the present. Here's an example: if you are thinking about what you are going to have for breakfast tomorrow, right now, this is thinking at the conscious level.

You have a hundred percent control of your conscious mind, if you allow yourself. The problem is many people are not aware of this and they allow any thought

He who conquers himself is the mightiest warrior.
                                    ~ *Confucius* 551-479 B.C.

enter their conscious mind; i.e. negative television pro-gramming, negative lyrics from songs, and even tabloids, just to name a few.

The dominant conscious thoughts that you let into your conscious mind eventually end up in the subconscious mind. The subconscious mind recycles all the thoughts from your conscious mind; this happens when you are awake or asleep. These are the thoughts that appear to pop out of nowhere. It is your subconscious mind that determines your beliefs about the world or your perception of it.

He who reins within himself and rules passions, desires, and fears is more than a king.

~ *John Milton* 1608-1674

How to Develop the Habit of ...

Self-mastery

STEP ONE

Meditation is one of the best ways to program your subconscious mind. Find a quiet spot in your home where you will not be disturbed. Sit in a lotus position (left leg crossed with left foot under right thigh, right leg crossed with right foot resting on left thigh) with your spine erect and head straight. Inhale through your nose for a full five seconds. When you inhale, make sure you feel your stomach expand. Exhale slowly through your mouth for seven to eight seconds.

Begin with five repetitions. You will start to feel relaxed shortly after you begin. Visualize the kind of person you want to become, see yourself doing the kinds of activities this ideal person would be doing. Create in your mind the feeling of having achieved the goal you are currently working on. You may want to do this for five to ten minutes initially, and gradually increase your meditation time so you may visualize all of your goals. See yourself achieving your five, ten and twenty year goals. This exercise, if practiced regularly, will create incredible momentum and optimism in your life.

The mind is like an iceberg, it floats with one-seventh of its bulk above water.
~ Sigmund Freud 1856-1939

STEP TWO

After you have finished step one, end your meditation with motivational affirmations which are consistent with your vision of your own higher self…your true self.

Listed below are a few of my favorite affirmations:

- Today I will appreciate the gift of life at all times, and I will be grateful for all the abundance in my life.

- Today I will live with passion by acknowledging that I am only here for a brief time and time is a commodity too precious to waste…not even for one second.

- Today I will tap into my strength, which comes from a higher source.

- Today I am creating abundance and prosperity for my family, my clients, and everyone with whom I come into contact.

- Today I am wiser than yesterday, because I have learned from yesterday's lessons and I am applying the wisdom of those lessons in my life right now.

Please use the above to start your own list of affirmations; it will make your meditation more powerful once you have added your own ingredients.

Nurture your mind with great thoughts, for you will never go any higher than you think.

~ *Benjamin Disraeli* 1804-1881

Try this exercise for twenty-one days. You will begin to feel calmer about life, have more focus and be well on your way to self-mastery. More importantly, you will have a deeper appreciation of the power of self-suggestion and it's role in self-mastery.

The highest possible stage in moral culture is when we recognize that we ought to control our thoughts.

~ *Charles Darwin* 1809-1882

A man who dares to waste one hour of his
life has not discovered the value of life.

Charles Darwin 1809-1882

Mastering Time

Now that you have designed your mission statement, written your goals, and constructed a plan to achieve your goals, it is time to go out and begin creating your life, the life you were meant to live.

The problem for many of us is that we get off track. We begin, full of enthusiasm and determination for the first few weeks. Slowly, but surely, we start to drift back to the same old habits. To be time effective, we must value time as we value any other precious commodity like gold or silver. When we value time we are less likely to squander it, on things such as watching too much television. The U.S. *News & World Report*, has stated that we will spend five years of our lives standing in line. I've read other reports that say the average American will spend seven years of their life watching television.

To be healthy, wealthy and wise, you must have strong time management skills. Time management is not complicated; you just need to implement an easy-to-use system to guide you through your short, medium and long-term goals. I have a formula to help you develop these skills, and it is quite simple.

You wake up in the morning, and your purse is magically filled with twenty-four hours of un-manufactured tissue of the universe of your life! It is yours. It is the most precious of possessions. No one can take it from you. And no one receives either more or less than you receive.   ~ Arnold Bennett 1867-1931

There are many time organizers on the market today. They show the months, weeks and days of the year, and can provide the structure you need to keep you moving forward. The following steps to successful time management will make achieving your life goals, on a consistent basis, substantially less intimidating.

- Regular review
- Prioritize your goals
- Block off time
- Regular follow up

Time stays long enough for those who use it.
~ *Leonardo Da Vinci* 1452-1519

How to Develop the Habit of ...

Mastering Time

STEP ONE

REVIEW REGULARLY Pick a specific time of the day, week, month, and year to write and review your daily, weekly, monthly, and yearly goals. For example, on a day that is unique to you, like your birthday, you may want to write your goals for the year ahead and review your goals from the previous year. Review the "Goal Setting" chapter. You may decide to write your monthly goals on the last Sunday of each month. If you do decide to write your monthly goals on a Sunday, I would also advise writing your weekly goals on the same day as well.

It does not matter which day you write and review your goals, just be consistent. Your daily goals should be written and reviewed at the same time each day. Review those goals at the beginning or the end of the day; it depends on whether you are a morning person or a night owl.

STEP TWO

PRIORITIZE YOUR GOALS Whether you are writing your goals for the day, week, month or year, (or any time in between) the first step is to list all of the tasks, errands,

Time is the most valuable coin in your life. You and you alone will determine how that coin will be spent. Be careful that you don't let other people spend it for you.

~ John Dryden 1631-1700

commitments and any other responsibility that will be called "goals" for that particular time frame.

Next, prioritize your list of goals into three categories; A-must do, B-should do and C-could do. Finally, go through each category and write a number beside each goal according to its priority. When you have completed numbering your A, B, and C priorities, you have prioritized your goals, and you will have a format to follow. For example, you would not start an A3 goal before completing your A1 and A2 goals.

STEP THREE

BLOCK OFF TIME After you prioritize your goals, turn to your organizer and block off time in the day, week or month, for all of your A goals first, followed by your B and C goals. Make sure you block off the most time to accomplish your A goals first, followed by your B and C goals.

STEP FOUR:

REGULAR FOLLOW UP It is almost impossible for most of us to accomplish all of our daily and weekly goals 100% of the time. We all have, from time to time, unavoidable interruptions that temporarily take us off track. Each day, follow up with your previous day's goals and carry forward those that you did not have time to complete to the current day. The same strategy should be employed for your weekly goals. If you faithfully follow this strategy your

Time is like money, the less we have of it to spare the further we make it go.
    ~ *Josh Billings* 1815-1885

monthly goals will be much easier to accomplish, as will your yearly ones.

Ralph Waldo Emerson wrote, "One of the illusions of life is that the present hour is not the critical, decisive hour. Write it on your heart that every day is the best day in the year. No man has learned anything rightly, until he knows that every day is Doomsday."

Follow these basic time management steps and watch what you'll be able to accomplish and how your health, wealth and wisdom will grow!

Time is Too slow for those who wait, Too swift for those who fear, Too long for those who grieve, Too short for those who rejoice. But for those who love, time is not.

~ Henry Van Dyke 1852-1933

Whatever you have spend less.

Samuel Johnson 1709-1784

Saving and Investing

"Money isn't everything" — what a terrible cliché! To me it's like saying "Health isn't everything." It makes no sense. Obviously money is not everything without health, happiness, peace of mind, and a purpose for being. However, in our civilized world money is very important. Although money, on its own, cannot make anyone happy, it does make life a lot more comfortable.

A very important part of being healthy, wealthy and wise is being wealthy. For the purpose of this book wealthy will be defined as having enough money to do what you want when you want. It is my belief that anyone can achieve wealth if the desire for wealth is backed up by a realistic plan.

Listed below are my "Nine Common Sense" investment and money management strategies for acquiring and preserving wealth:

1. Buy Mutual Funds. In my opinion mutual funds are one of the most responsible ways to invest for your retirement or to maintain and preserve your wealth at retirement. At the time of this writing the Nasdaq stock market, in the United States, is down sharply from the 2000 year high, many investors just lost a

It is, generally, in the season of prosperity that men discover their real temper, principles, and designs.

~ Edmund Burke 1729-1797

substantial portion of their retirement savings by trying to pick individual stocks themselves. Hire a professional — sleep well at night!

2.   Save 20% of what you earn. Invest most of it, but always keep some handy for a rainy day. The rule of thumb is to keep three to six months earnings readily available.

3.   Spend less than you earn. With credit and financing being so accessible today it is easier than ever to spend more than you earn. Today, in North America the savings rate is at the lowest it has been in decades and far too many of us will not have enough savings for retirement unless we change our spending habits.

4.   Buy life insurance. If you live in any of the G7 Nations you may pay a lot of money in taxes. Granted these countries are nice places to live, but their taxes are very high — at death as well. A solid life insurance policy will insure that your loved ones will have enough money to pay estate taxes and preserve the integrity of the estate.

5.   Hire a financial advisor. Work with a financial advisor that has access to a variety of investment products like mutual funds, bonds, stocks and annuities. Ask a few of your trusted friends if they are happy with the

The fortune which nobody sees makes a person happy and unenvied.
~ *Francis Bacon* 1561-1626

results they are getting with their financial advisor. If they are, ask them if they would mind referring him/her to you. Always ask for references and interview at least three advisors. Pick the one you trust.

6. Pay off your debts. A person free from debt will probably never know poverty. Debt is the reason for many marriages breaking up; it can put too much pressure on the relationship. If you develop a habit of living within your means you will never be a prisoner of debt.

7. Dollar cost average in mutual funds. Since 1896, the stock market (Dow Jones Industrial Average) has had several bear markets and corrections and has still managed to give investors a cumulative price return of just over 17,000%. A common sense strategy I recommend is to invest a fixed amount every month. That way, when the market goes down you buy more, and when the market goes up you buy less. In the long run your average cost on your mutual fund investments will be lower than those who invest a lump sum at the beginning of each year.

8. Own your own home. Why pay rent and finance someone else's mortgage payments when you can build your own equity? Each month you pay rent is another month of lost equity in your own future. When it's

The highest use of capital is not to make more money, but to make money do more for the betterment of life.

~ *Henry Ford* 1863-1947

time to sell your primary residence, if there is a realized gain on the sale, the first $250,000 in profit is tax free in the United States per individual or $500,000 if you are filing a joint return. In Canada there is no tax to pay!

9. Hire an Accountant. In addition to analyzing your cash flow needs, an accountant can advise you on ways to reduce the amount of taxes you pay. Since this is a complex area, take advantage of the experts available to assist you with your tax planning strategies. These strategies cover maximizing tax credits and eligible deductions, adopting tax-smart investment ideas, deferring taxes to the future and many more.

If money be not thy servant, it will be thy master. The covetous man cannot be said to possess wealth, as that may be said to possess him.
~ Francis Bacon 1561-1626

How to Develop the Habit of ...

Saving and Investing

STEP ONE

Invest a small percentage of your next pay. If you are just starting out, I suggest you begin with a *very* small amount. The goal is to develop the habit of saving and investing; odds are you won't miss five percent of your pay. Again, mutual funds are a great way to invest. Sit down with your financial advisor and pick a fund that suits your risk tolerance and your time horizon. (For clarity and peace of mind I recommend you read the fund's prospectus before investing.)

Every month you will be buying a lump sum of mutual funds. After a while you won't notice the payments, but within a short time you will be amazed as your wealth grows every thirty days. Gradually increase your monthly contributions to twenty percent of your pay. For some, especially those with young families, this number may be impossible; if so, don't worry, as long as you are investing every month you are developing an "abundance mentality."

HEALTHY, WEALTHY & WISE ————————————

Neither a borrower, nor a lender be: For loan oft loses both itself and friend, And borrowing dulls the edge of husbandry. This above all: to thine own self be true, And it must follow, as the night the day, Thou Canst not then be false to any man. ~ *Shakespeare* 1564-1616

TAKE THE HEALTHY WEALTHY AND WISE ABUNDANCE TEST™

Listed below are twenty questions, which will help evaluate your Wealth Creation and/or Wealth Depletion habits. For every yes answer give yourself 5 points, for every no answer don't give yourself any points.

The Healthy Wealthy and Wise Abundance Test™

1. Do you invest a fixed amount of money on a regular basis?
2. Do you avoid buying items on credit (charge cards) when you can pay cash instead?
3. Do you not lose sleep when the stock market is going through a correction or a bear market?
4. Do you actually get excited about all the bargains in the stock market when it has a correction or goes through a bear market?
5. Have you hired a financial advisor to help you create and maintain a path to wealth?
6. Have you had a retirement income projection prepared for you, to let you know how you are doing financially?
7. Do you regularly update your retirement income projection, to make sure you are staying on track?
8. Have you actually sat down to make a list of your monthly and yearly expenses?

HEALTHY, WEALTHY & WISE

Beware the little expenses; a small leak will sink a great ship.

~ *Benjamin Franklin 1706-1790*

9. Have you made some minor or major improvements to your monthly and yearly expenses which will increase your wealth?

10. Have you written clearly defined goals to create wealth on a short (1-5 year), medium (5-10 year) and long term (20 years plus) basis?

11. Do you have an *abundance mentality*? In other words, do you think that you deserve to be wealthy?

12. Do you fully expect to be wealthy?

13. Do you currently possess *an attitude of gratitude*? (If you are grateful for all the abundance you currently are receiving, no matter how small, you are more likely to attract abundance.)

14. Do you help others less fortunate than yourself in any way? For example, do you volunteer for a charity or a worthwhile cause? (Volunteering or giving to a worthwhile cause will make you feel like a billionaire!)

15. Do you let strangers go before you on the highway, on the subway, in line at the bank, or in line at a movie? (This habit builds an *abundance mentality* by acting as if there is enough to go around. Added bonus ... you will feel fantastic!)

16. Do you give more than is expected of you in your work, with your relationships, and with yourself? The hand that gives is the hand that gathers.

17. Do you currently visualize yourself in possession of the wealth which you desire?

HEALTHY, WEALTHY & WISE ⎯⎯⎯⎯⎯⎯⎯⎯⎯⎯⎯⎯⎯⎯⎯

Without a rich heart, wealth is an ugly beggar.
                    ~ *Ralph Waldo Emerson* 1803-1882

18. Do you currently own your own home or are you planning on buying in the near future?

19. Have you hired an accountant to help you reduce the taxes you pay?

20. Do you have enough life insurance to meet your family's needs?

How to analyze your results:

If you scored 80-100 points you are well on your way to becoming wealthy. You have an abundance mentality and are well disciplined with your investing and saving habits.

If you scored 60-75 points you have a good foundation for creating wealth, but you do need to make a few adjustments. It may be you need to spend less on unnecessary grocery items (junk food) or maybe you could tone down your transportation needs. In the case of the latter, automobiles are meant to be used as a mode of transportation; it's the advertising which creates the illusion that an expensive automobile will make you appear successful. Don't misunderstand me, if you have more than enough wealth I am all for a nice car. Unfortunately, too many people are driving cars that are not within their "real" budget. These are the people who have too much month left at the end of the money.

That some should be rich, shows that others may become rich, and, hence, is just encouragement to industry and enterprise.
~ *Abraham Lincoln* 1809-1865

If you scored under 55 points you are on the right path — you took the test. However, you have a few wealth depletion habits that must be eliminated before you can start creating wealth. Hopefully, this test pointed out your weak points. Take action today! Write down a plan to address your wealth depletion habits. I suggest you start small. Like saving and investing, the key is to actually start and develop the habit that will put you on the road to financial wealth.

The gratification of wealth is not found in mere possession or in lavish expenditure, but in its wise application.
                                        ~ *Miguel De Cervantes* 1547-1616

Resources

To assist you with your quest to become Healthy Wealthy and Wise I have listed some resources for you to refer to when you need some inspiration or some supplies for your journey. These resources include some great web sites to visit for further learning, as well as Healthy Wealthy and Wise approved company web sites; these sites offer products and services specifically designed to help you get to where you want to go! Here they are:

Franklincovey.com
A great site for time management products.

Wayne Dyer's Meditations for Manifesting
A great audiocassette, which offers a very user-friendly technique for learning how to meditate.

The Organized Executive Newsletter.
A wonderful time management newsletter with terrific ideas. For subscription information call 703-518-2345.

Feel the Fear and Do It Anyway
Susan Jeffers, Ph.D. A great audiocassette or book on learning how to take risks.

What to Say When You Talk To Your Self

Shad Helmstetter One of the best written books I've come across that offers easy to understand yet powerful information on methods to control your thoughts and control your life. Do the exercises in this book…you'll love the results.

Nightingale.com

The Nightingale-Conant Corporation has all the latest material for sale from the greatest authors in the world. You'll find information on everything from business, health and wellness, spiritual growth, wealth building and more.

Success Magazine

A great magazine for entrepreneurs, offering timely advice on sales & marketing, new business ideas, motivation and more. For more information go to successmagazine.com.

Oprah.com

Inspired by the "Oprah Winfrey Show" this site has tons of great articles on inspiration, healthy recipes, mind and body, relationships and more.

Selfgrowth.com

A self improvement weekly newsletter. This newsletter offers its subscribers weekly information on self improvement and personal growth as well as related products and services.

Great Life Today

A wonderful newsletter from greatlifenetwork.com that offers life-changing content from the world's foremost authorities on life-leadership

Jimrohn.com

Jim offers a free weekly email publication which offers words of wisdom on everything from self improvement, time management, relationships, business success and more. Jim has been in the personal development business for decades. He offers rock solid advice on improving the quality of life.

Suggested Reading List

For a car, train, plane or any other kind of machine to run efficiently and to maximize it's life, we know that we must put good things into them and provide regular maintenance. Good things like premium fuels, high calibre parts, and regular tune ups help these machines get the "most out of life."

We, too, need to put good things into ourselves to get the "most of out life." In order for our minds to grow, our ideas to expand, our wealth to grow and our quality of life to improve we need to be continuously learning. I have given away most of the books I have read on personal development over the years, but I have saved and refer to often, what I feel are some of the best books/audio cassettes written on improving the quality of life. Some of these authors must be listened to, rather than just read. You'll want to hear Leo Buscaglia's passion for life in *Celebrate Life*; reading this information is great but I believe listening to the authors conviction, enthusiasm and excitement in their message is even better!

Here are some of my favorites:

On Self Improvement

> **As a Man Thinketh**,
> James Allen (book)

> **The Magic of Believing**,
> Claude Bristol (book)

> **Think and Grow Rich**,
> Napoleon Hill (book or audio)

> **Wisdom of the Ages**,
> Dr. Wayne Dyer (audio)

> **Celebrate Life**,
> Dr. Leo Buscalia (audio)

> **Who Will Cry When You Die**,
> Robin Sharma (book)

> **Manifest Your Destiny**,
> Dr. Wayne Dyer (book)

> **Personal Power**,
> Anthony Robins (audio)

> **Quantum Leap Thinking**,
> James J. Mapes (audio)

On Time Management

The Seven Habits of Highly Effective People,
Dr. Stephen R. Covey (audio)

The Organized Executive,
Stephanie Winston (audio)

How to Manage Time and Set Priorities,
Stephen Young (audio)

On Goal Setting

**Goals, Setting and Achieving Them on
Schedule**, Zig Ziglar (audio)

The New Dynamics of Goal Setting,
Denis Waitley (audio)

On Relationships

Men are From Mars, Women are From Venus,
Dr. John Gray (audio)

A Couple's Guide to Communication,
Dr. John Gottman (book)

On Investing

Manias, Panics, and Crashes,
Charles P. Kindleberger (book)

The Millionaire Next Door,
Thomas J. Stanley, Ph.D. and
William D. Danko, Ph.D. (book)

The Wealthy Barber,
David Chilton, (book)

Simple Wealth, Inevitable Wealth,
Nick Murray (book)

On Creating your Mission in Life

Now, Discover Your Strengths,
Marcus Buckingham and
Donald O. Clifton, Ph. D. (audio)

The Law of Success,
Napoleon Hill (book)

On Spiritual Growth

The Seven Spiritual Laws of Success,
Dr. Deepak Chopra (audio)

Applying the Wisdom of the Ages,
Dr. Wayne Dyer (audio)

The Art of Happiness,
His Holiness The Dalai Lama
and Howard C. Cutler, M.D. (audio)

How to Know God,
Pantanjali

About the Author

Derrick R. Sweet is Founder and Chairman of The Healthy Wealthy and Wise™ Corporation, a progressive international company which specializes in *Life Improvement* seminars and keynote speeches. In his presentations, Derrick talks about the true meaning of wealth, as it applies to the mind, body and soul. He also teaches strategies to create and implement abundance in our personal life and career, as well as common sense investment strategies.

At the age of 38, Derrick retired from a distinguished career as Vice President and Senior Investment Advisor of a large investment firm to focus 100% of his time on speaking about the powerful message of *Healthy Wealthy and Wise*.®

Clients include Fortune 500 companies, large associations, financial services firms, government agencies and major health-care institutions. To learn more about The Healthy Wealthy and Wise Corporation please visit healthy-wealthyandwise.com or call toll free (Canada and the United States) 1-866-455-2155.

ABOUT THE HEALTHY WEALTHY AND WISE CORPORATION

Seminar/Keynote Speech Division

The Seminar/Keynote Speech Division specializes in life improvement seminars and keynote speeches. Our mission is to teach leading corporations, government organizations and major associations about the true meaning of wealth, as it applies to the mind, body and soul. We educate our clients on strategies which will allow them to create more joy, peace of mind and prosperity in all the important areas of a well balanced life. We are especially renowned for our *Get the Most Out of Life* presentations (based on Derrick Sweet's book of the same name) where we teach our clients all the "little" things we can do *everyday* to live with more passion, purpose and contribution! Our speakers and trainers are all personally trained by Derrick Sweet. For more information please call 1-866-455-2155 or visit www.healthywealthyandwise.com

Wealth Creation Division

The Healthy Wealthy and Wise Corporation offers a very unique business opportunity for individuals seeking to work part time or full time in an environment where they can promote, market and distribute the best information on topics related to Health, Wealth and Wisdom, including; fitness, exercise, diet, investing, retirement planning, tax reduction strategies, time management, goal setting techniques, relationships, motivation and inspiration. We offer an attractive compensation package for individuals who are seeking an opportunity with a progressive, fun and exciting wealth creation corporation. For more information please call Derrick Sweet at 1-866-455-2155 or e-mail him at dsweet@healthywealthyandwise.com or visit www.healthywealtyandwise.biz

Get the Most Out of Your Next Event, Conference or Internal Training Program!

Derrick Sweet is known as a truly gifted speaker who speaks from his heart on what we can all do to live in the realm of our higher self, create internal wealth,make a significant contribution, live with a greater sense of purpose and truly *Get The Most Out of Life!*
His hearty laugh, sense of humor and ability to inspire his audiences to new heights are distinct trademarks of an unforgettable experience with Derrick Sweet.
To find out why Derrick's presentations are in such demand by Fortune 500 companies, major financial institutions, large associations and government agencies, please call David Aaron at 1-866-455-2155 or e-mail him at info@healthywealthyandwise.com

"Derrick Sweet is a truly wonderful individual; a positive outlook humor and enthusiasm are of utmost importance in life and Derrick exudes these qualities in the presentation; his synergy with the participants is amazing! His integrity and authenticity are refreshing. His hands-on approach was simple to understand and easy to integrate into one's daily life. His ideas help us focus on our goals and develop a new way of seeing life."

Francois Duguay,
Learning Centre Administrator, Rogers Communications Inc.

We want your feedback

Derrick R. Sweet would appreciate hearing from you.
Please write us with the insights and successes that you
have enjoyed as a result of reading a particular chapter
or practicing an exercise in this book.
We would love to hear from you!
Please write to Derrick R. Sweet, c/o:

The Healthy Wealthy and Wise Corporation
1 Yonge Street, Suite 1801
Toronto, Ontario
M5E 1W7

E-mail: derricksweet@healthywealthyandwise.com

HEALTHY WEALTHY AND WISE

ORDER FORM

Give the gift of abundance! Could someone in your life benefit from the philosophy of *Healthy Wealthy and Wise*™? It's the ideal gift for clients, friends, and relatives. It's also a perfect gift for your organization to give as a thank you to your existing clients or as an incentive with sales campaigns for future clients.

Please rush me_____copies of *Healthy Wealthy and Wise*™ at $15.95 Canadian or $9.95 in U.S. funds each, PLUS $5.00 CDN shipping and handling. I have enclosed a cheque made payable to **The Healthy Wealthy and Wise Corporation** in the amount of:

$_____ (Cdn.) or $_____ ((U.S.)

Full Name: _____

Address: _____

_____

Province/State: _____ Postal Code/Zip Code: _____

Telephone #: _____

E-mail address (optional): _____

Please send funds to:

The Healthy Wealthy and Wise Corporation
1 Yonge Street, Suite 1801
Toronto, Ontario M5E 1W7

To order 50 books or more please call toll free (Canada and the United States) 1-866-455-2155 or 416-410-9990 to inquire about our corporate discounts.

PLEASE ALLOW THREE TO FOUR WEEKS FOR DELIVERY.

Lifetime Guarantee

I am so confident in the philosophy of *Healthy Wealthy and Wise*™ that if, for any reason, you are not 100% completely satisfied with the information in this book, I will send you a complete refund if you return this book with your proof of purchase.

Return to:

The Healthy Wealthy and Wise Corporation
1 Yonge Street, Suite 1801
Toronto, Ontario M5E 1W7

This guarantee is for life. The information in this book is powerful. It will help you create abundance in your life. For this to happen you must practice every exercise in every chapter and you must participate in the exercises with faith and an open mind. You will get results.

NOTES

NOTES

NOTES